E-MAIL
What It Is and How to Use It

Enslow Publishing
101 W. 23rd Street
Suite 240
New York, NY 10011
USA

enslow.com

Tricia Yearling

WORDS TO KNOW

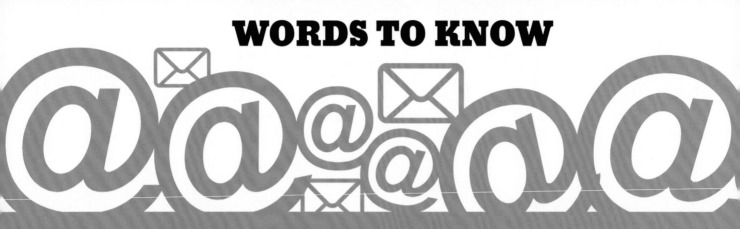

compose—To write.

e-mail—Short for electronic mail; a message, note, or letter you send through the Internet.

emoji—A symbol created in text that actually looks like the emotion it represents.

emoticon—A series of punctuation and letters that are meant to represent emotions.

forward—A method of sending an e-mail to another person. Sometimes this is a message, a picture, or even a video that was sent to you first, then you send it to someone else.

inbox—Where your unread e-mail messages are held.

reply—To respond to someone's e-mail or message. There is also an option to reply all, which means if there is more than one person in the e-mail, they will all see your response.

server—A computer program that stores and presents web pages.

spam—An e-mail that has been sent out to many people, which is usually an advertisement, and the sender does not know the recipient in person.

store-and-forward—A method of writing, sending, receiving, and saving messages between friends on the Internet.

subject—The main topic of your e-mail. It could be as simple as "Hi" or even an emoticon like :) .

virus—Just like in your body, this is an illness a computer can catch that is sometimes sent through spam. It can slow down the computer or make it stop working altogether.

CONTENTS

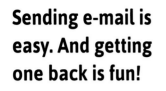

Sending e-mail is easy. And getting one back is fun!

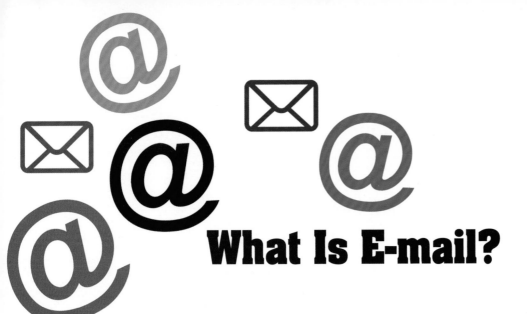

What Is E-mail?

You may have heard adults talking about checking their e-mail. What is e-mail? Why do you have to check it? Well, similar to the way that you must check your mailbox to see if you have any letters, you must check your inbox to see if you have any e-mails.

E-mail is a method of sending messages to friends or loved ones through the Internet. People often use e-mail to keep in contact with people who are far away. Through e-mail, you can easily talk to your grandmother in Florida or your cousin in Oregon!

Messages Through the Internet

E-mail is a simple, environmentally friendly way to communicate, especially with people who live far away or in a different time zone. If you have access to a computer, smartphone, or tablet, e-mail is available for you.

Sending an e-mail to your friend is much quicker than writing a letter. An e-mail arrives almost immediately!

In the 1860s, the United States was expanding, and people were moving out West. They wanted to keep in contact with family and friends back East. So the Pony Express was created. Riders on horseback would gallop at top speed to get letters back and forth between settlers and the cities they left behind. The Pony Express ran for only one year, but it delivered approximately 35,000 letters!

A Brief History of E-mail

Many people depend on e-mail today. But there certainly wouldn't be such a thing as e-mail without mail! People have been sending letters to each other since the invention of the written word. Letters and other mail were sent by messengers on foot or horseback. Eventually, letters were sent by train or steamboat. But in the 1800s, the first e-mail was sent.

Electronic Messages

The telegraph is a machine that used electricity to send short messages across long distances. Telegraph operators used a system called Morse code, which is an alphabet made from a series of clicks and pauses. You could even call these messages the first text messages!

In the 1800s, telegraphs were the fastest way to get a message to someone far away. Telegraph operators were very important!

Modern E-mail

The first computers were so large that one computer took up an entire room. But as technology advanced, computers became smaller and easier to use. In the summer of 1971, a computer expert named Ray Tomlinson sent the first e-mail. It was sent between two computers that were sitting next to each other on the same table.

Since 1993, e-mail has become more and more common. Nearly everyone seems to have an e-mail address now. And some people have more than one!

In 2004, the @ symbol got its own code in Morse:

·— —·— ·

Typing is essential for sending e-mails.

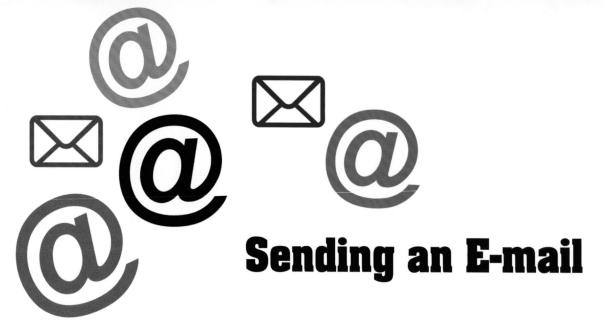

Sending an E-mail

In order to send an e-mail, you must first have an e-mail address. E-mail addresses are different than mailing addresses.

Setting Up an Account

Most e-mail servers will give you an e-mail address for free, and usually you can choose your own. A server is a computer program that stores and presents web pages on the Internet.

In order to get an e-mail address, you will have to create a username, or login, and a password. Your username should never give away any personal information, such as your name or birthday. Instead, it should be a nickname, something you're interested in, or your favorite color. For example:

purpleunicorn09@enslow.com

goalie123@enslow.com

keyplayer@enslow.com

Your password should always be something you can remember but not something someone else could guess.

Always have an adult help you set up your e-mail account. The @ symbol is very important. It means the word "at." So the e-mail address purpleunicorn09@enslow.com means that purpleunicorn09 can be reached "at" the server enslow.com. Common e-mail servers are AOL (@aol.com), Outlook (@outlook.com), Gmail (@gmail.com), and Yahoo (@yahoo.com).

E-mail is a store-and-forward method of communicating. This means that when an e-mail is sent, it is stored in a station in between the two computers. There, it is saved and kept until it arrives at its final destination. This sounds complicated, but the process only takes a few seconds.

The @ symbol means different things in different parts of the world. It is always used the same way in an e-mail address, but it is called something different in many languages. The Dutch call this symbol *apestaart*, meaning "monkey's tail." The Swedes call it *snabela*, which means "an A with an elephant's trunk." Italians call this symbol *chicciolina*, which means "small snail."

Writing an E-mail

After you have your e-mail account set up, it's time to write an e-mail! Most e-mail servers will have a Compose button on or near the upper left-hand corner. Some servers might say New Mail. Others might say New Message, but all these mean the same thing. If you click on that button, a window should pop up. This is a place for you to enter an e-mail address, a subject, and a message.

Adding Attachments

Besides the text of a message, you can also send people photos, videos, and documents, too. Most e-mail programs have an attachment option. Sometimes it has a picture of a paperclip. Just click on Attach File or the paperclip. A

16

new window will pop up. Click on photos or click to the folder your file is in by using a dropdown menu. Once you find what you want, click Open. Your photo or file will be attached to your e-mail.

After you have written or attached everything you'd like, all you have to do is click the Send button. Sometimes this button may be labeled with a paper airplane. On other servers it will be labeled Send. Once that's done, your e-mail is on its way!

You may also reply to a friend's message by clicking the Reply button. You can also forward the message, or send it to someone else. These are options that will be in the window when you are reading your message.

Different Kinds of E-mail

E-mail can be used to communicate with people over long distances. It is used to send friendly notes to friends or more formal messages.

You should never e-mail someone you don't know. Be sure to tell an adult if you start receiving messages from an unfamiliar address.

Casual E-mails

Sometimes e-mail is informal and friendly, like when you send a message to your friend. In these messages, you can say whatever you'd like. There is no right or wrong way to compose your message. Using emoticons, or punctuation and letters in patterns to make faces, is encouraged. Some emoticons include:

:)	happy	;)	winking face (usually used when joking)
: O	surprised		
: D	very happy or laughing	: /	unsure
:'(	crying	: P	tongue out, happy
: (	sad	: |	not sure what to say

It should be noted that an emoji is different than an emoticon. An emoji is a figure that looks much more realistic. Emojis can be anything from expressive faces to dancing ladies to pieces of fruit.

Unwelcome E-mails

Not all e-mail is welcome in your inbox. Sometimes, spam messages will wind up in your inbox. It is safe to assume that any message sent from an address you don't know is spam. Spam messages are often advertisements or other annoying messages. Do not open spam messages. These often contain viruses that will attack your computer. These viruses could get your personal information, slow down your computer, or even cause it not to function at all.

Sometimes these messages go into a special folder in your e-mail. That folder might be called Junk or Spam.

Most e-mail servers allow you to report spam. This will block that address from ever sending another message to your inbox. Otherwise, you should delete the message, which will put it in your trash. You can do this with e-mail conversations you are finished with, as well. Be sure to empty your trash regularly!

More than 294 billion e-mails are sent around the world every day! That's approximately 100 trillion e-mails a year, and 3.5 million every second!

Sometimes an e-mail from someone you know accidentally ends up in your junk or spam. You can move it back to your inbox or click something like "Not Spam."

Remember, never open an e-mail from an address or name you don't recognize. If one of these ever appears in your inbox, tell an adult immediately. They can help you decide if this message is worth opening or if it should be deleted.

E-mail is a fun way to stay in contact with friends and loved ones all over the globe. Ask an adult for help, and create your own e-mail account so you can start sending and receiving e-mails today!

Sending e-mail can be a lot of fun!

WRITE A FORMAL E-MAIL

Sometimes, you'll need to e-mail people such as teachers, distant relatives, coaches, or other adults. For these types of e-mails, you should write in a more formal, proper way.

1. A formal e-mail should begin with a proper greeting. "Dear Sir or Madam," "To whom it may concern," or "Good day," work well.

2. The subject line of a formal e-mail should always contain exactly what you're writing about. For example: "This month's practice schedule," "Recital next Sunday," or "Makeup homework for (date)."

3. After this, you should write in the main text your question, comment, or the purpose of your e-mail. Be direct and specific.

4. Then, close with a farewell remark, such as "Have a nice day," "I hope all is well," or some other sort of well wishes. Whenever appropriate, thank the person to whom you are writing and close with your name and contact information, such as your phone number—but only if it is a person you know personally. Ask an adult if you aren't sure.

LEARN MORE

Books

Heos, Bridget. *Be Safe on the Internet*. Mankato, MN: Amicus Publishing, 2015.

McHugh, Jeff. *Maintaining a Positive Digital Footprint* (**Information Explorer Junior**). Ann Arbor, MI: Cherry Lake Publishing, 2015.

Miller, Shannon. *Don't Talk to Strangers Online* (**Internet Do's & Don'ts**). New York: Powerkids Press, 2013.

Websites

mouse-mail.com/about
E-mail that's safe for kids.

pbskids.org/arthur/games/letterwriter/e-mail.html
E-mail explained for kids.

sciencekids.co.nz/sciencefacts/technology/computers.html
Fun facts about computers.

INDEX

Published in 2016 by Enslow Publishing, LLC.
101 W. 23rd Street, Suite 240, New York, NY 10011

Copyright © 2016 by Enslow Publishing, LLC.
All rights reserved.

No part of this book may be reproduced by any means without the written permission of the publisher.

Library of Congress Cataloging-in-Publication Data

Yearling, Tricia, author.
E-mail : what it is and how to use it / Tricia Yearling.
    pages cm. — (Zoom in on technology)
Audience: 5+.
Includes bibliographical references and index.
ISBN 978-0-7660-7367-8 (library binding)—ISBN 978-0-7660-7365-4 (pbk)—ISBN 978-0-7660-7366-1 (6pk)
1. Electronic mail systems—Juvenile literature. I. Title.
TK5105.73.Y43 2016
004.692—dc23
                2015034184

Printed in the United States of America

To Our Readers: We have done our best to make sure all website addresses in this book were active and appropriate when we went to press. However, the author and the publisher have no control over and assume no liability for the material available on those websites or on any websites they may link to. Any comments or suggestions can be sent by e-mail to customerservice@enslow.com.

Photos Credits: Cover, p. 1 VIGE.CO/Shutterstock.com; Flat Design/Shutterstock.com (@ backgrounds and headers throughout book); p. 4 Monkey Business Images/Shutterstock.com; p. 6 mervas/iStock/Thinkstock; p. 7 Solodov Alexey/Shutterstock.com; p. 9 Marzolino/Shutterstock.com; p. 11 marcoscissetti/iStock/Thinkstock; p. 13 Dejan Stanisavljevic/Shutterstock.com; p. 15 Lisa S./Shutterstock.com; p. 24 Monkey Business Images/Shutterstock.com.